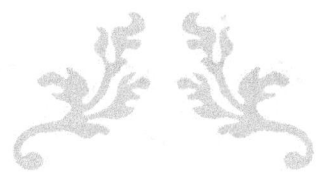

IMPRESSIONS OF NATURE
COLORING BOOK

by Shirley Burge

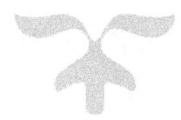

EZZBE DESIGNS

PECUALIAR, MO

Notes from the Author

It's time for some "you time" and relax.

Forget all the hustle and bustle of the everyday things and spend some alone time creating with me. I love sketching and creating these images and can't wait to see what your colored versions look like. So get out your crayons, colored pencils, markers etc. and start personalizing these images.

I would love for you to share your versions with me so please feel free to like and post completed versions on the EzzBe Designs Facebook page
https://www.facebook.com/ezzbedesigns?ref=aymt_homepage_panel I am always open to new ideas and suggestion, please feel free to share those with me.

Thanks for your interest, I hope you enjoy coloring these as much as I have sketching them.

Happy Coloring!

Inspiration

These illustrations have been inspired by watching nature from my home, motorcycle rides and various photographs from various sources on the internet.

Thank You

Thank you to my loving man. I couldn't do any of the things I do without your love, patience and support. Love you with all I am Scott Brown!

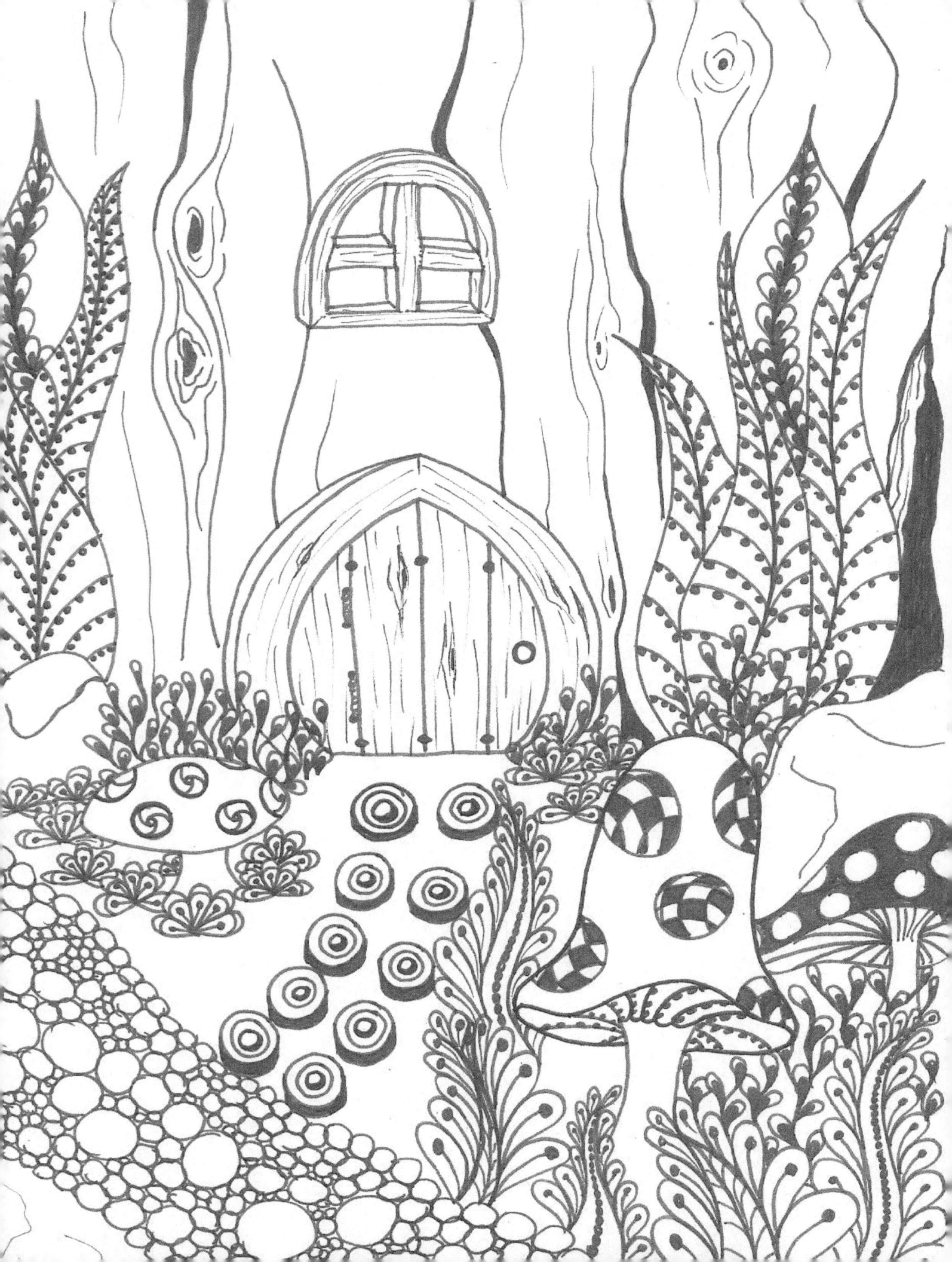

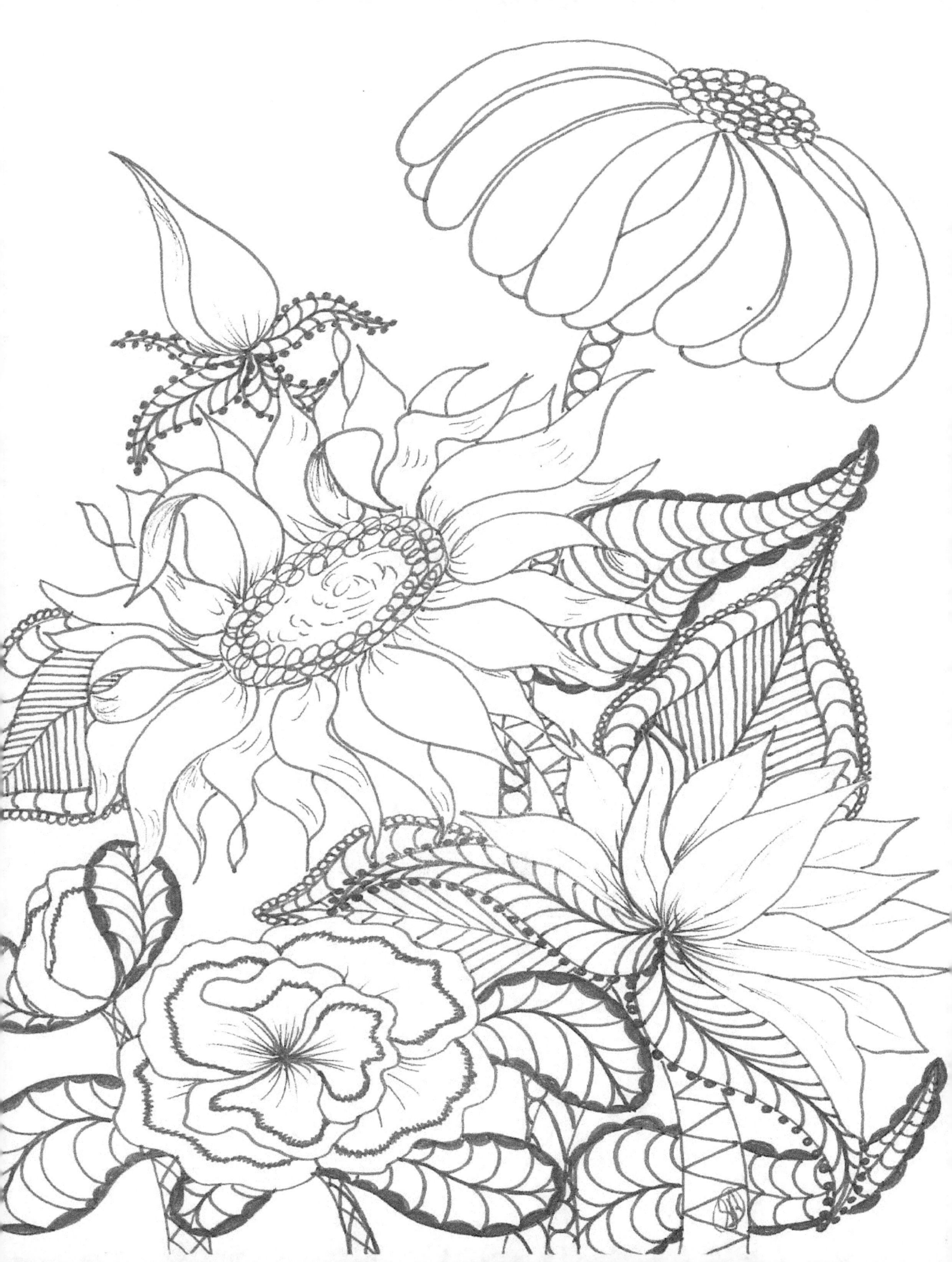

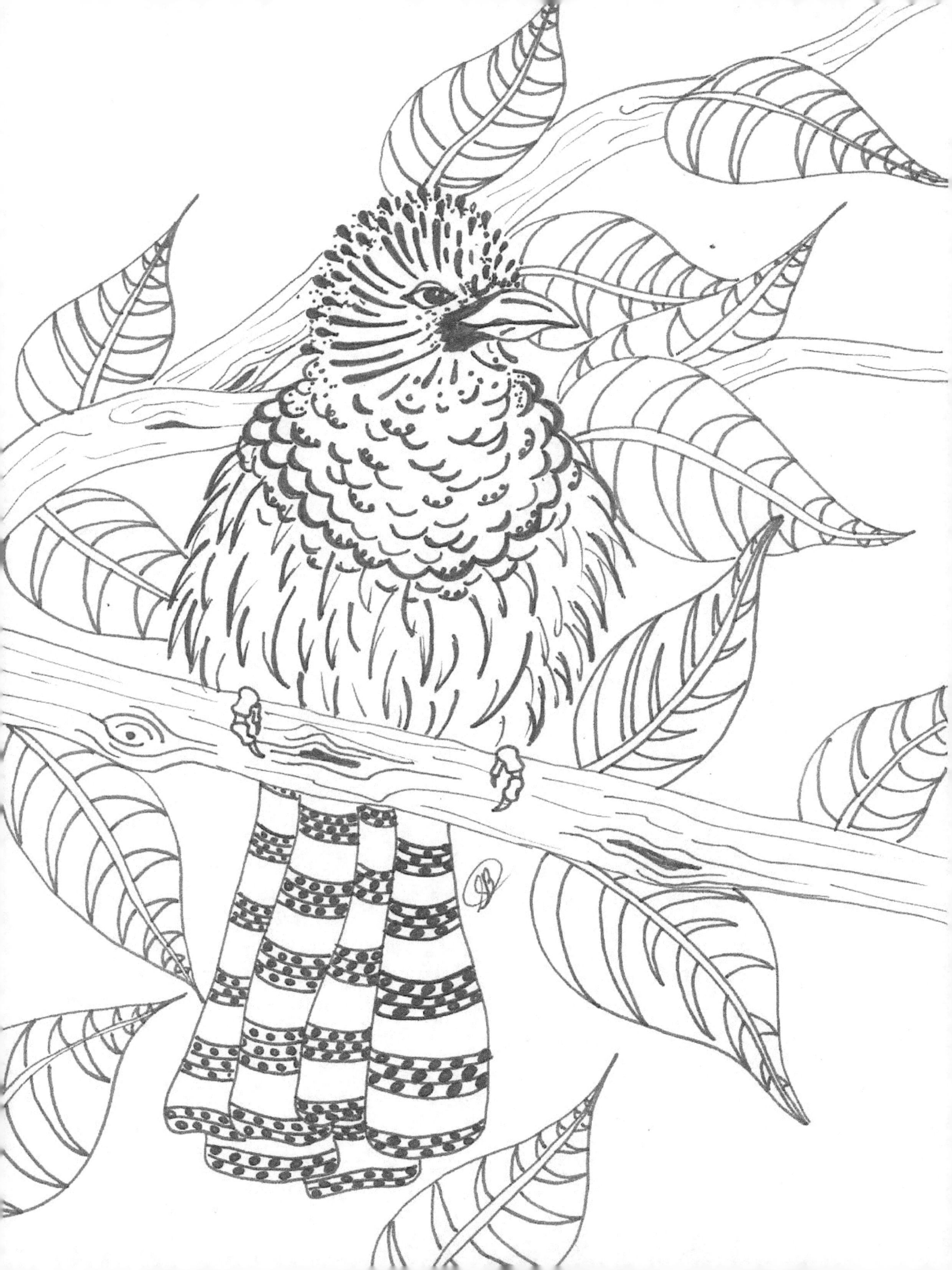

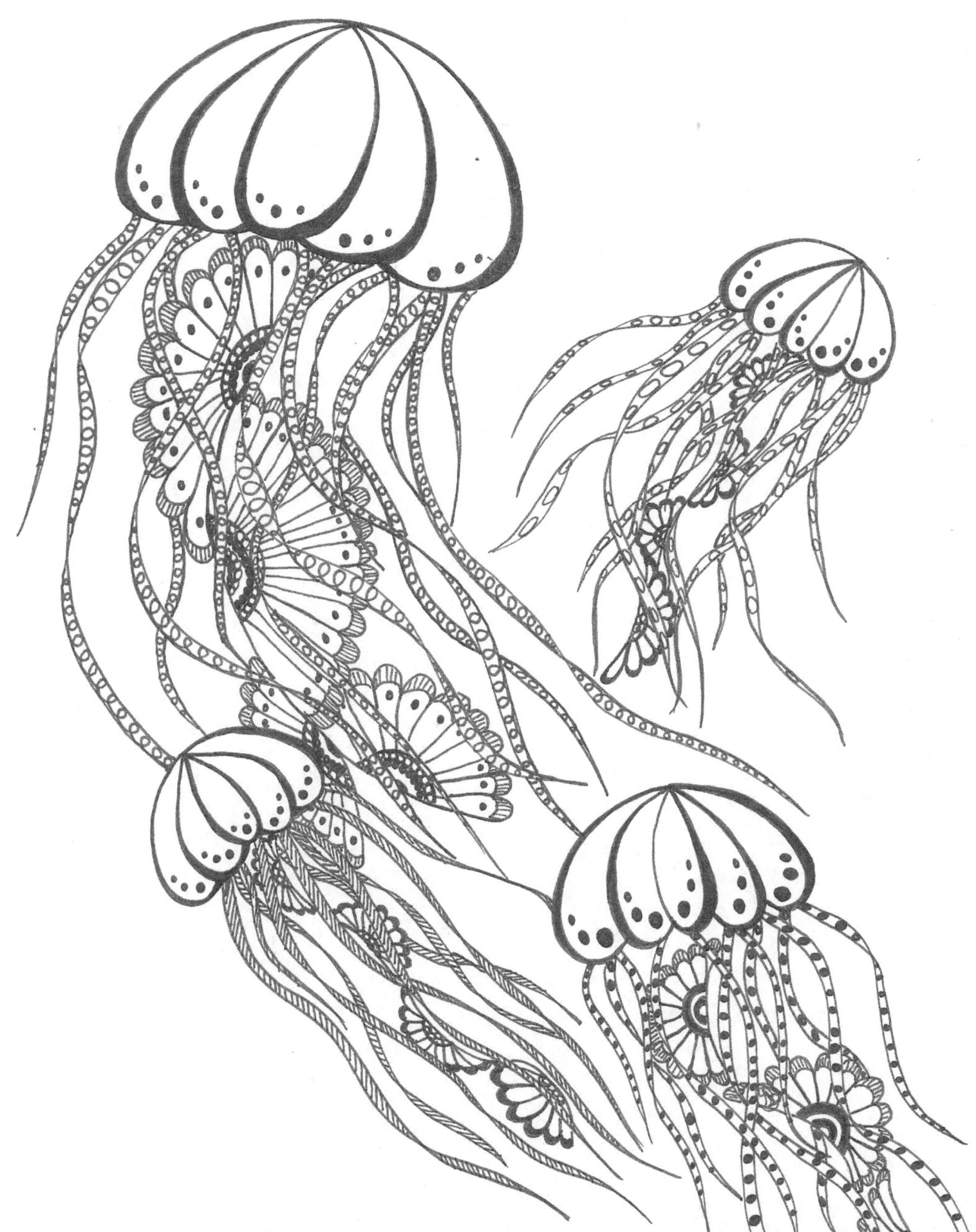

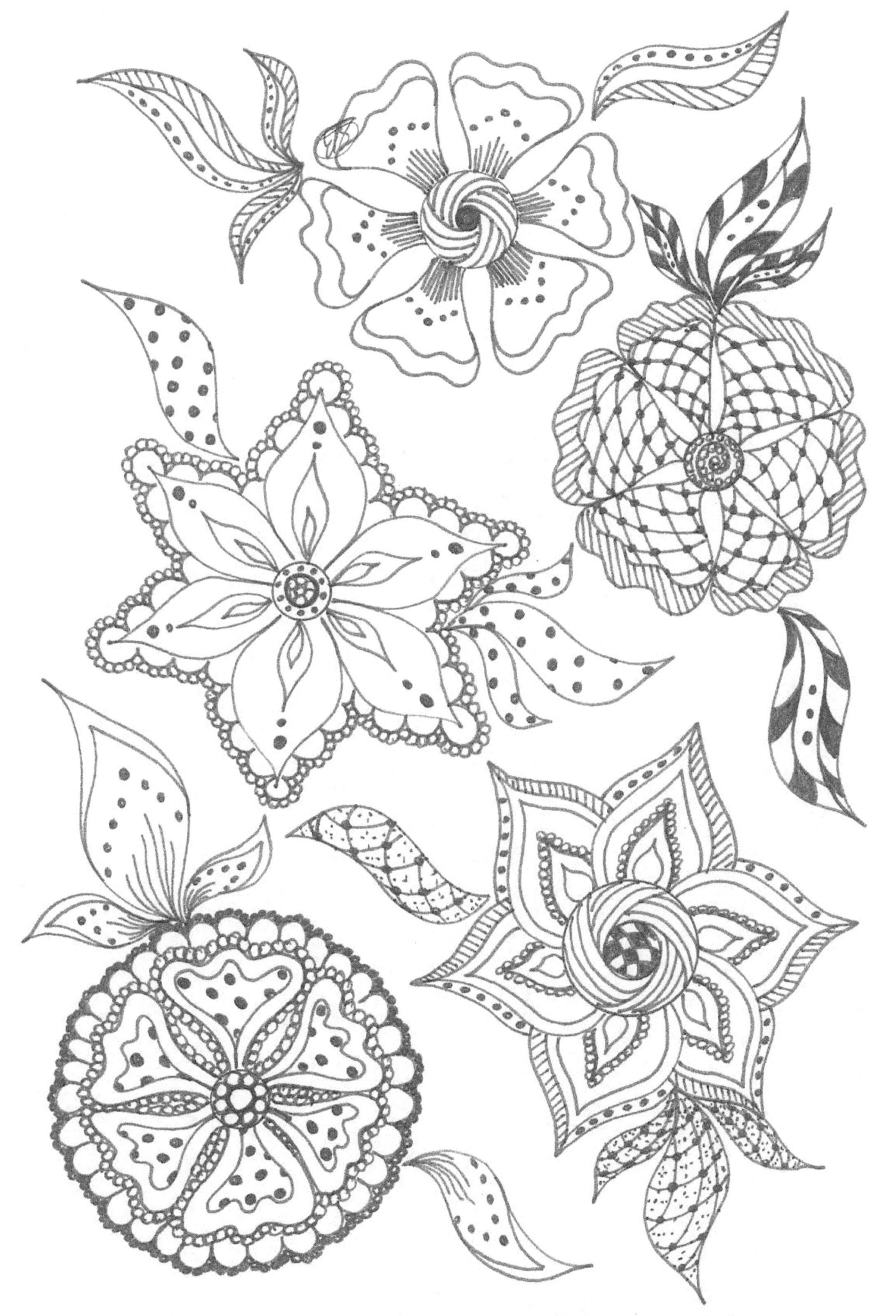

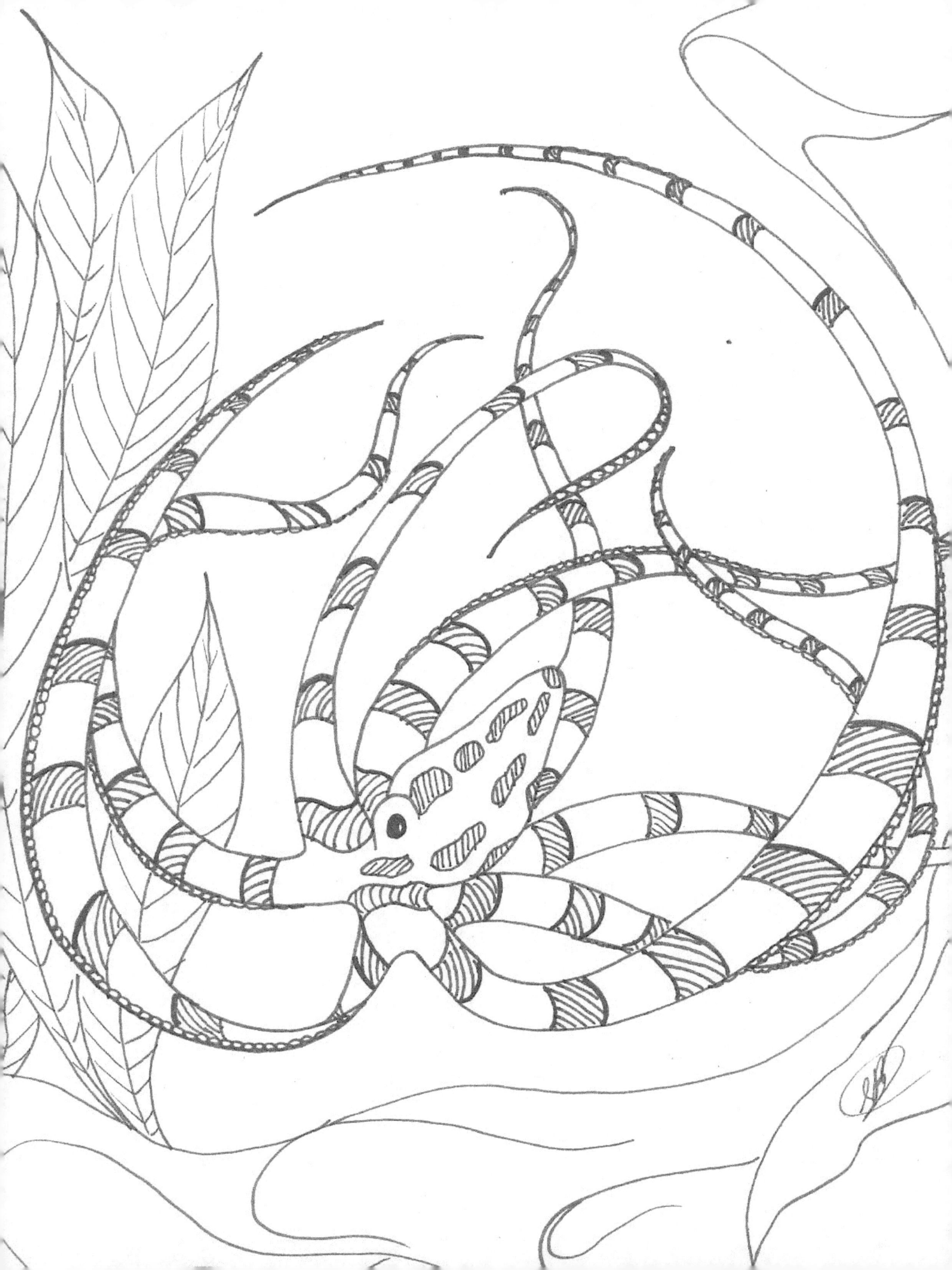

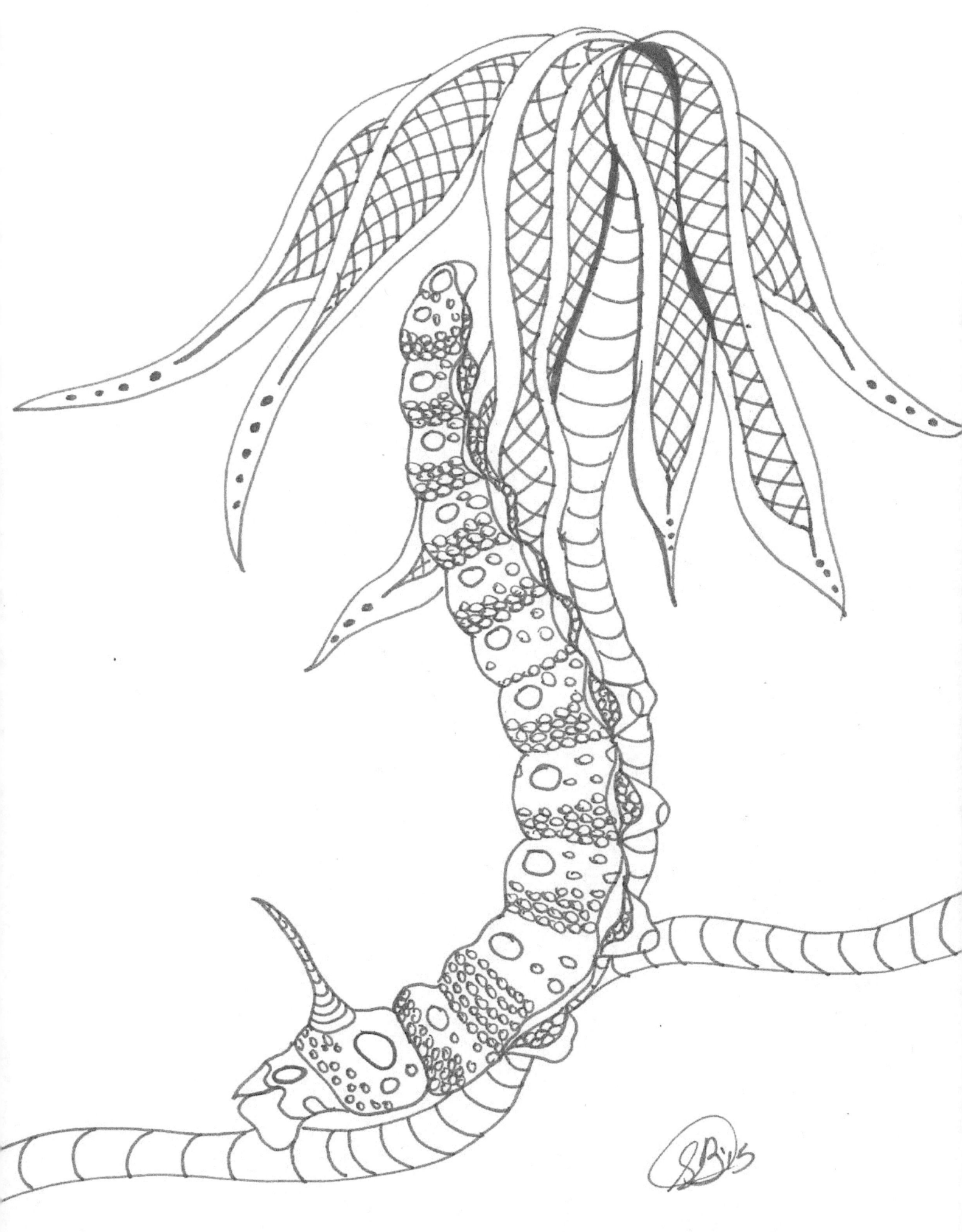

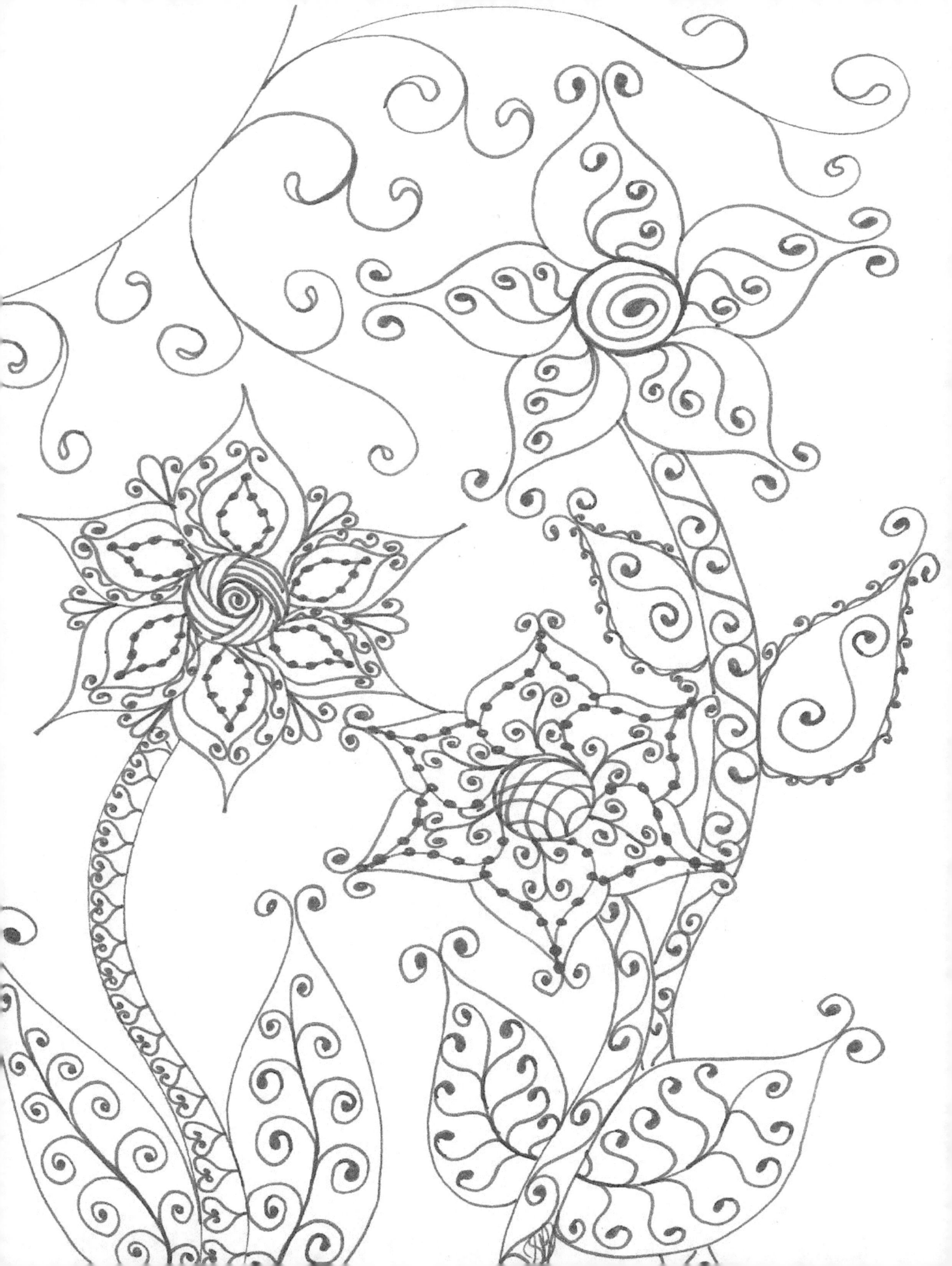

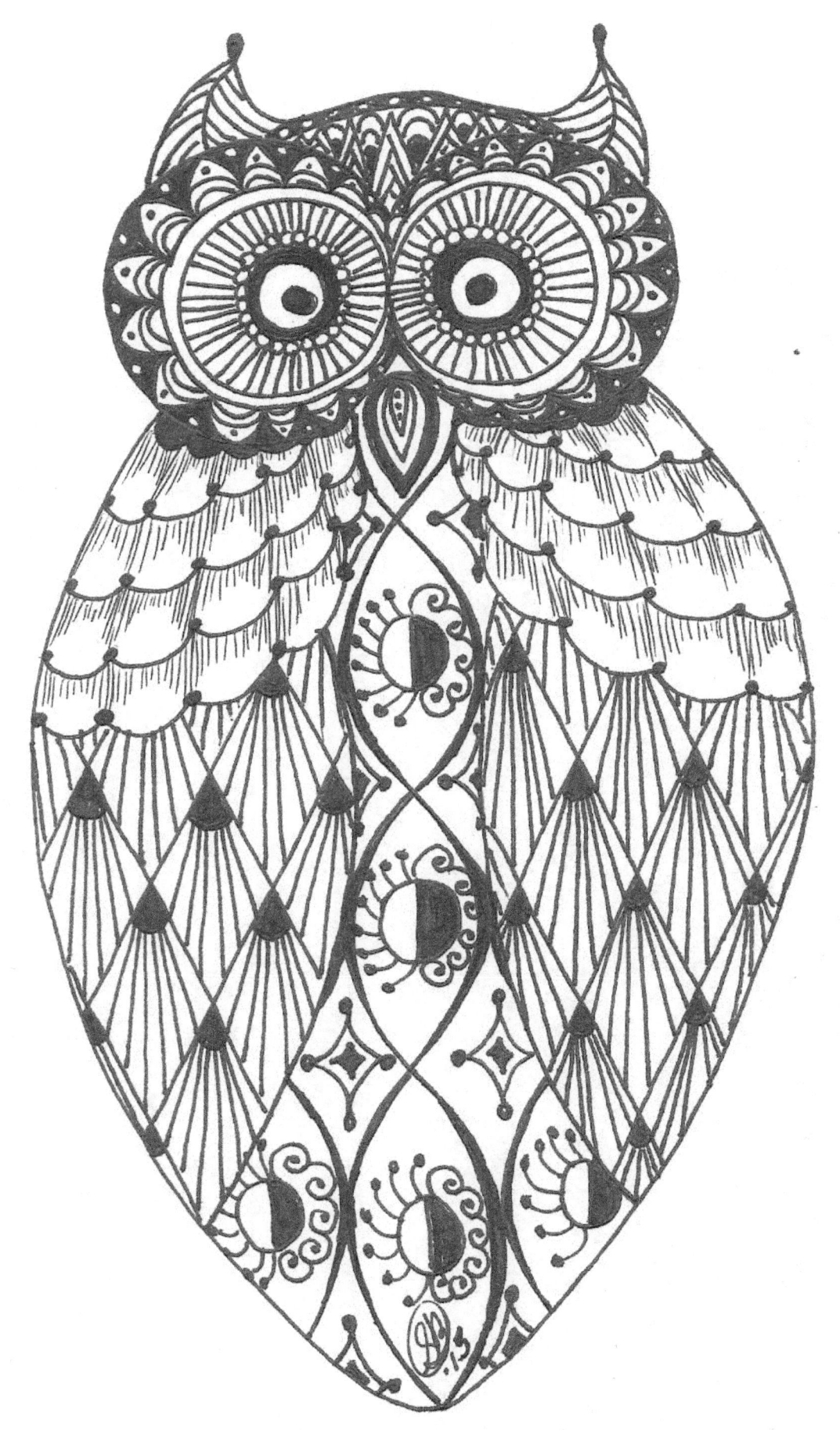

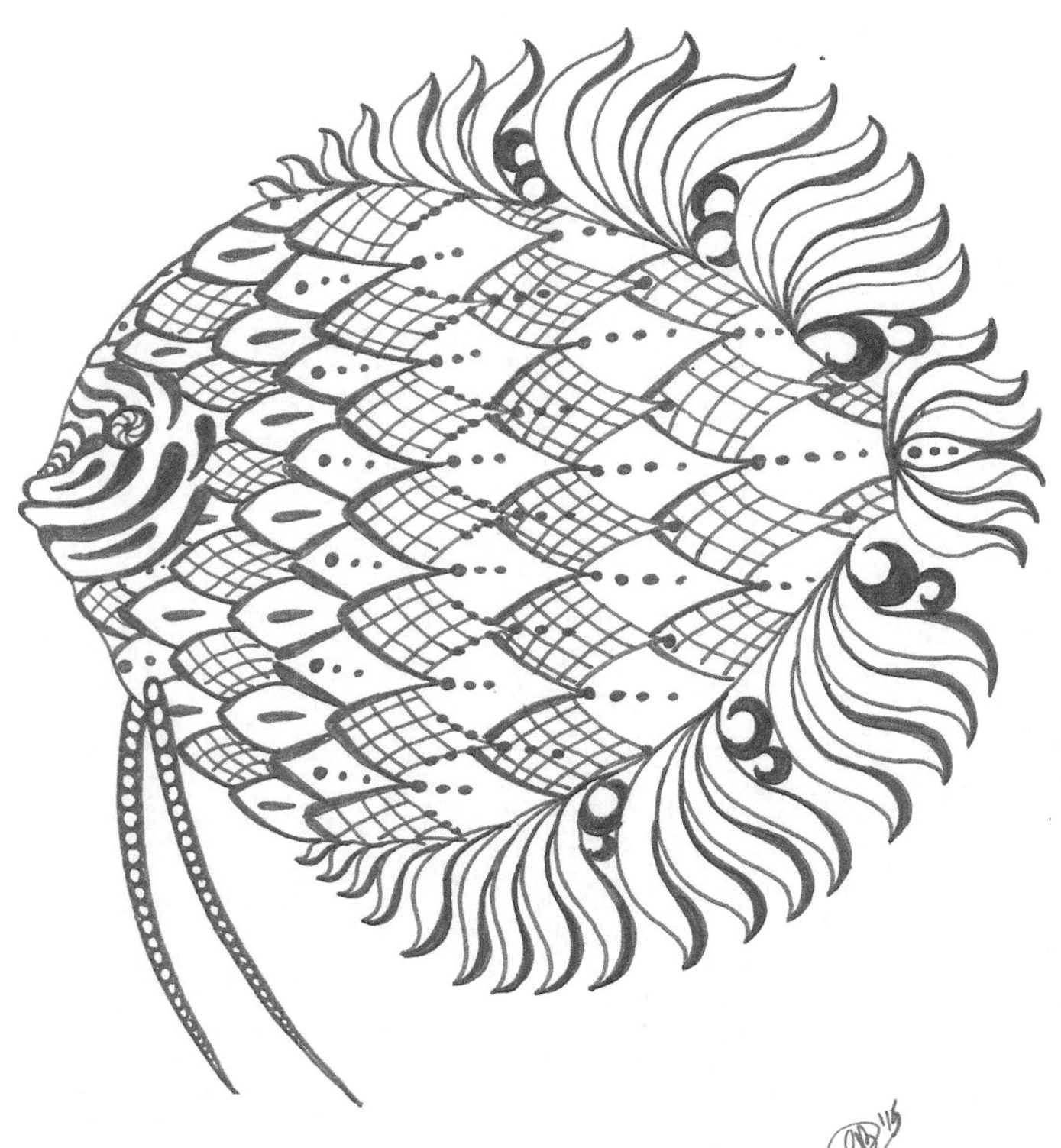

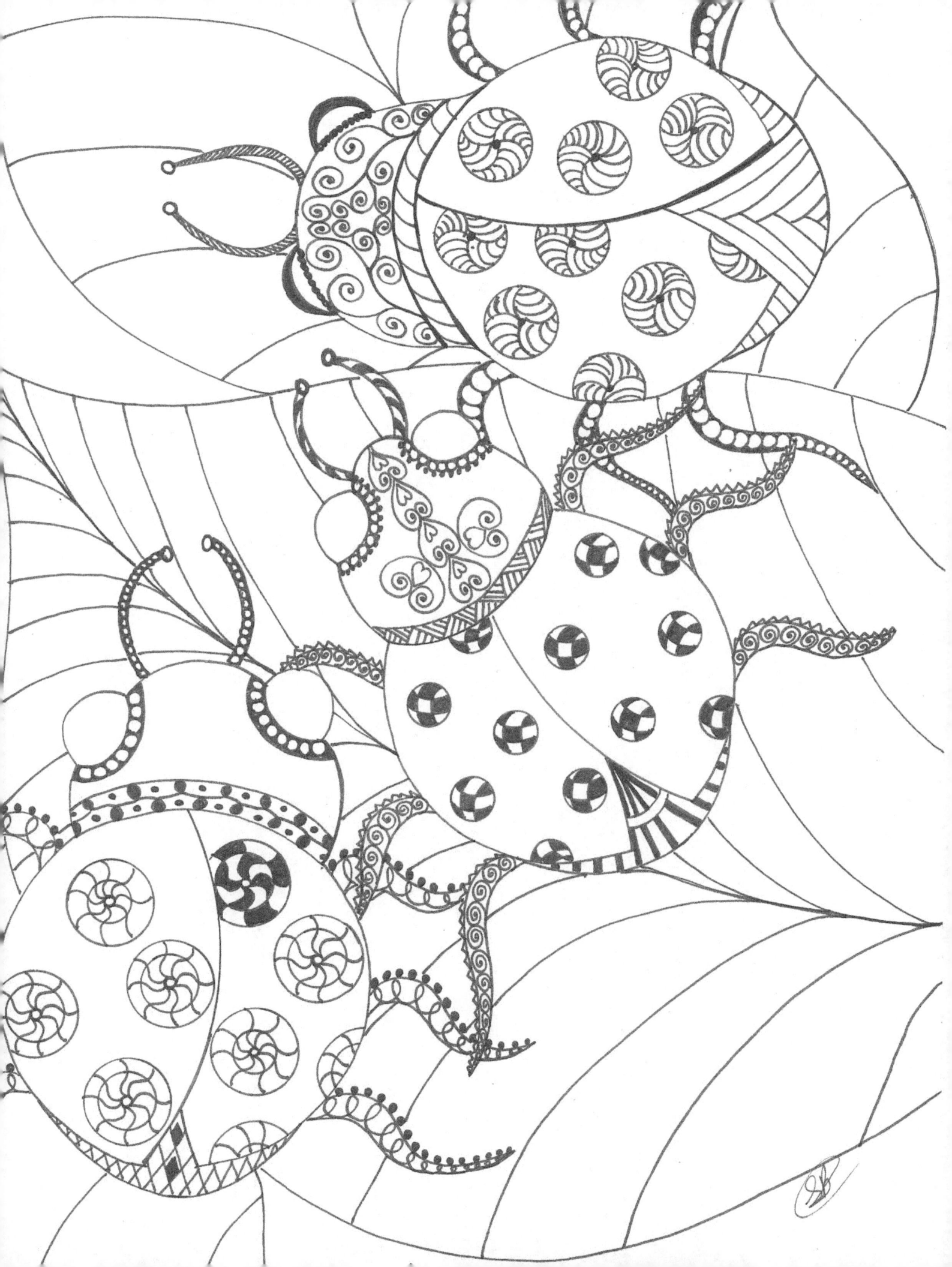

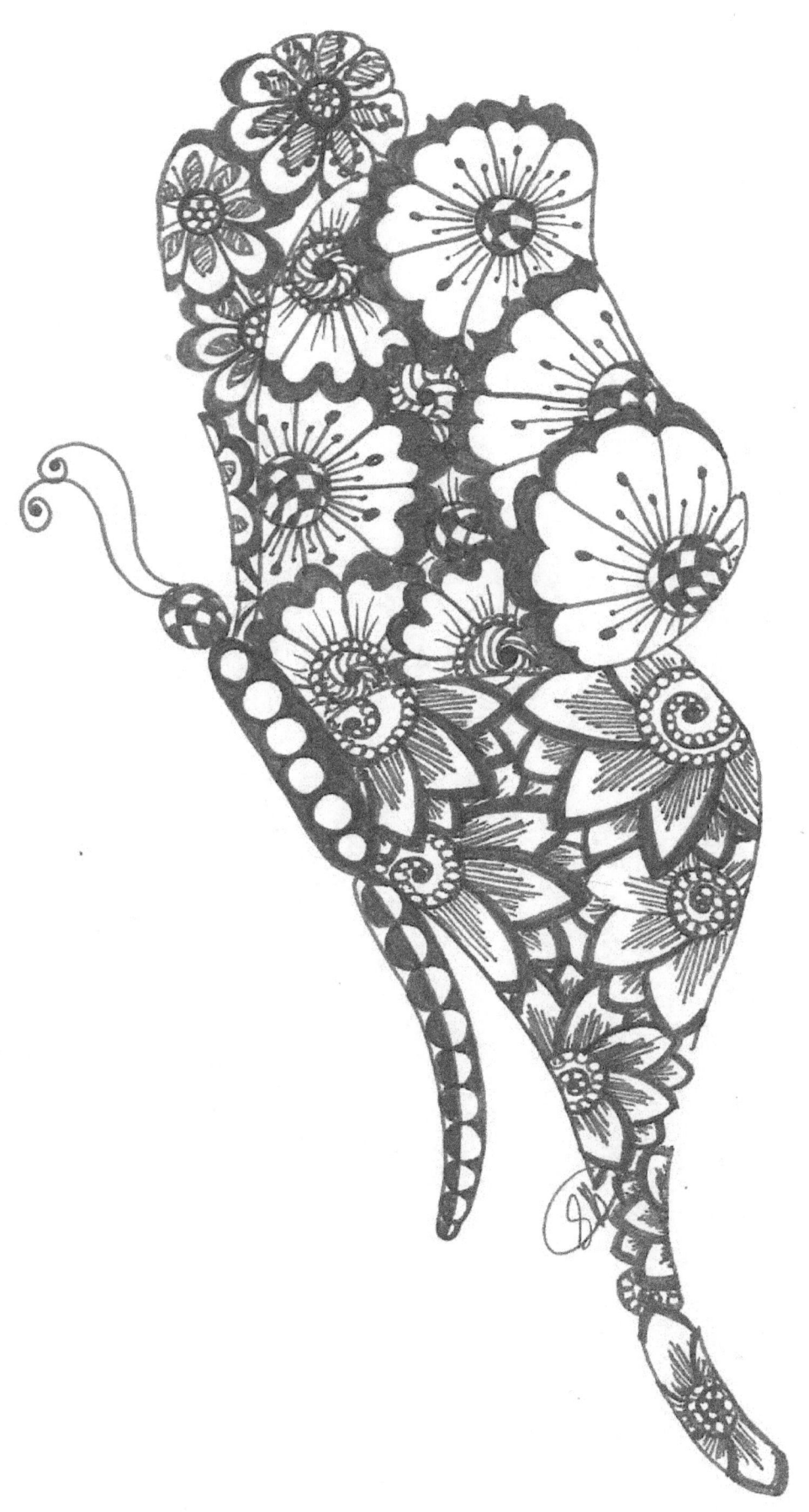

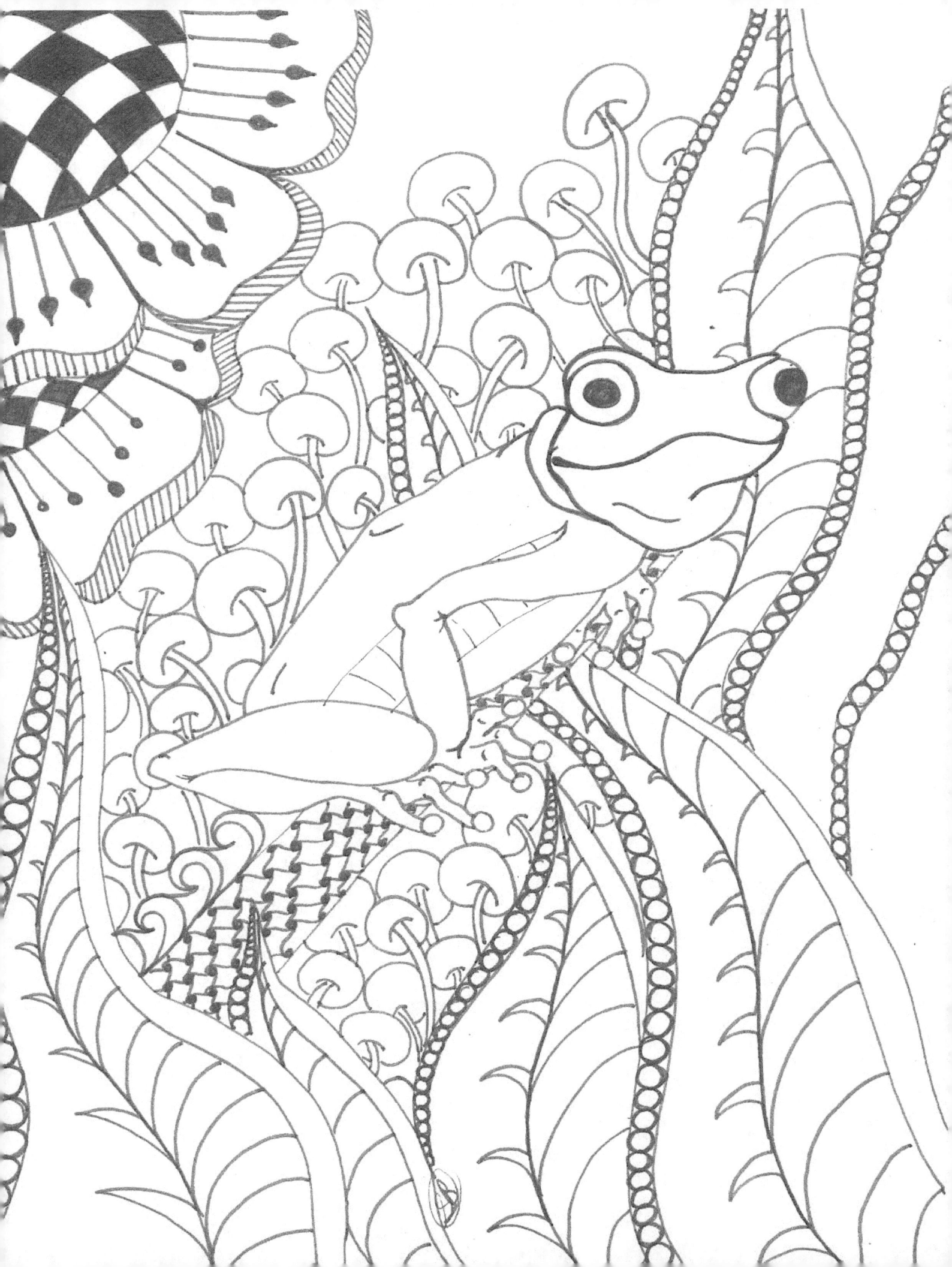

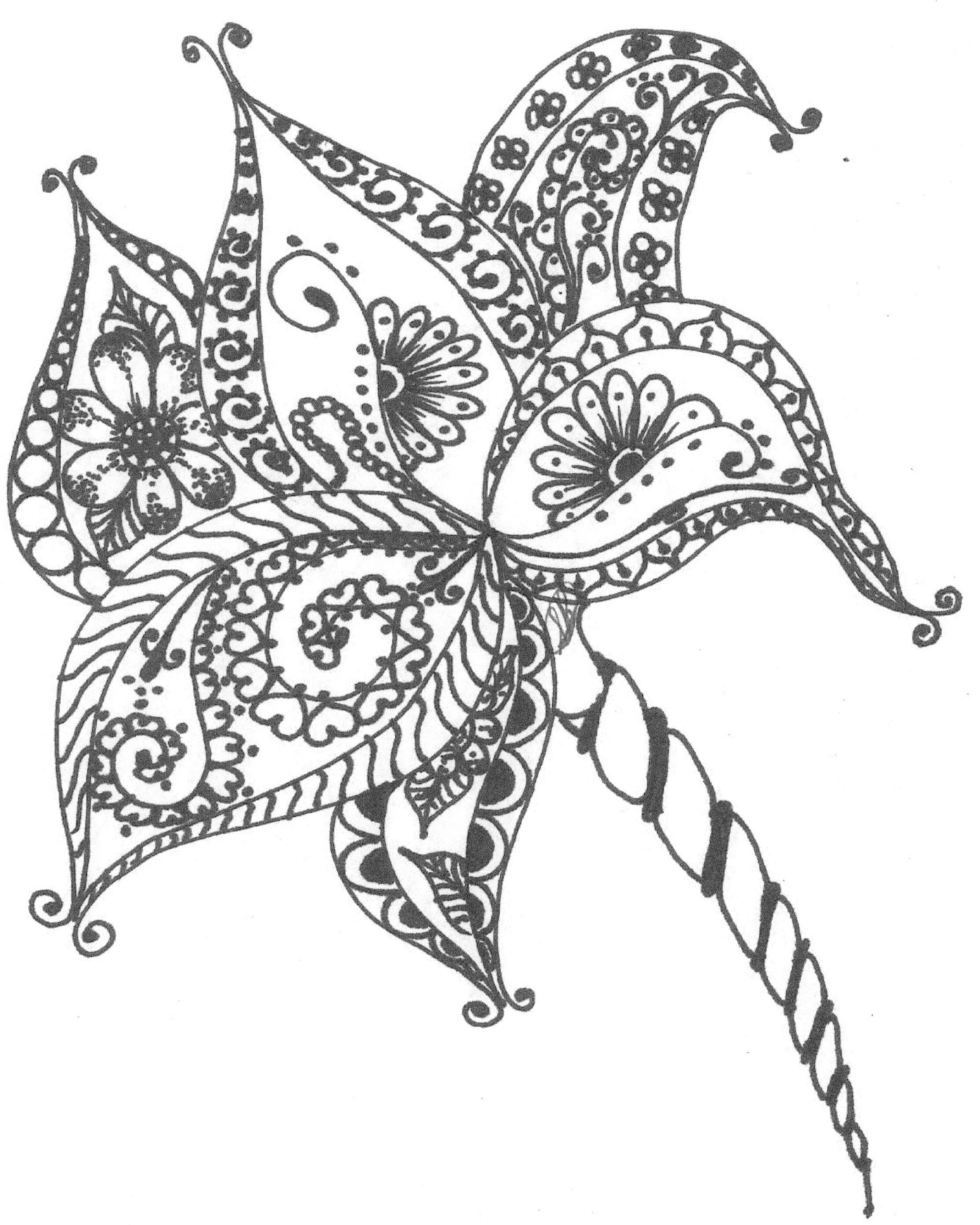

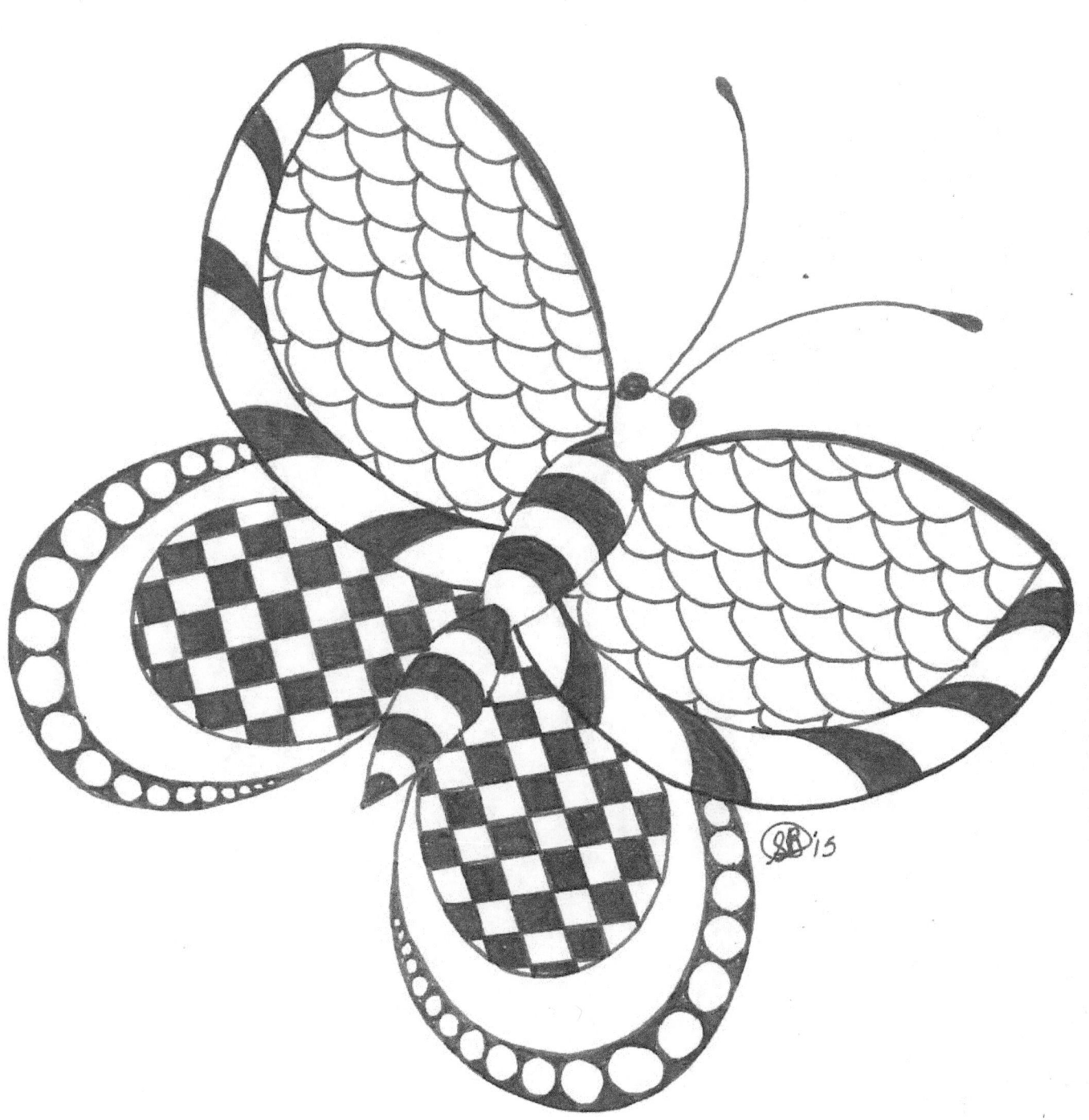

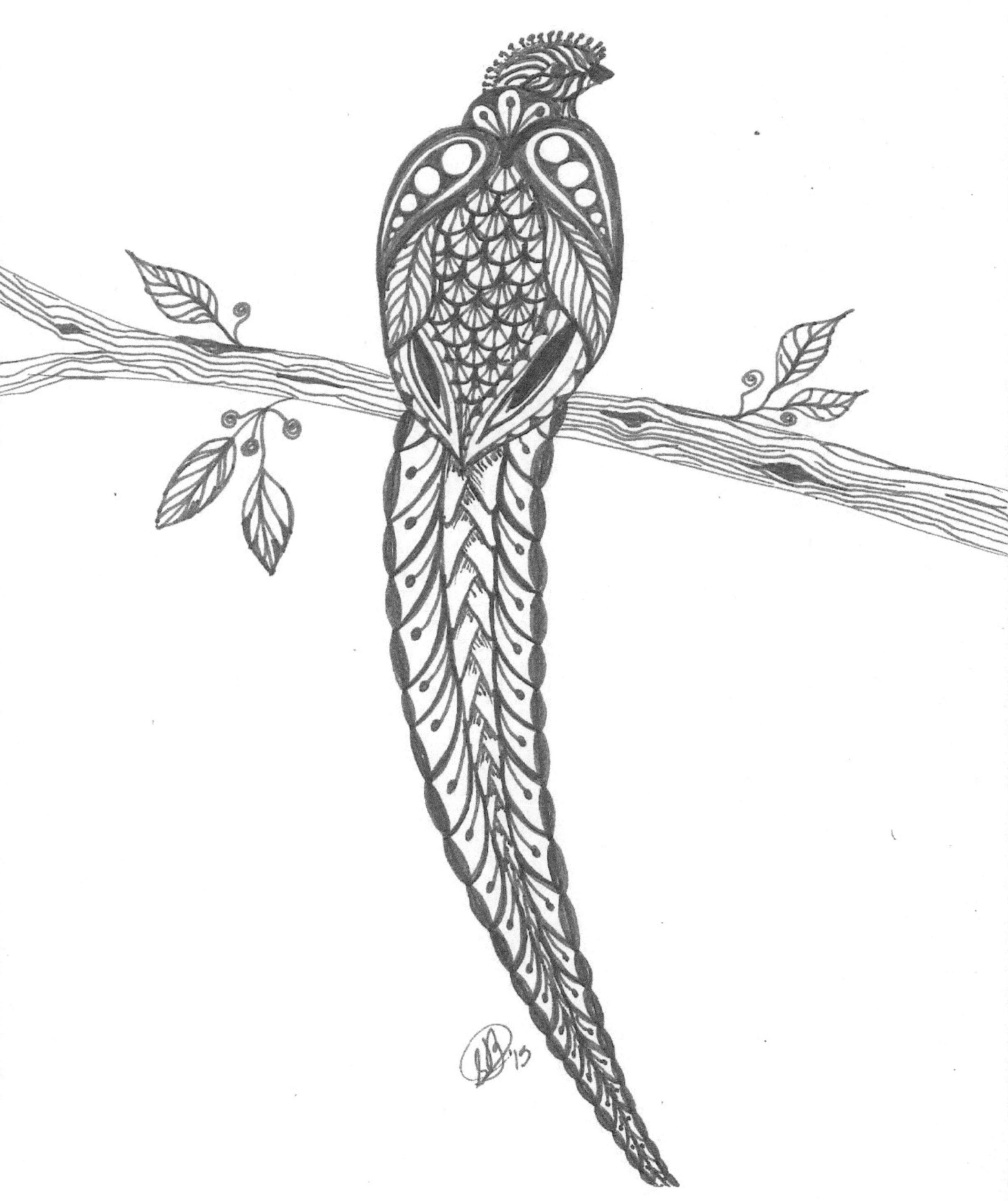

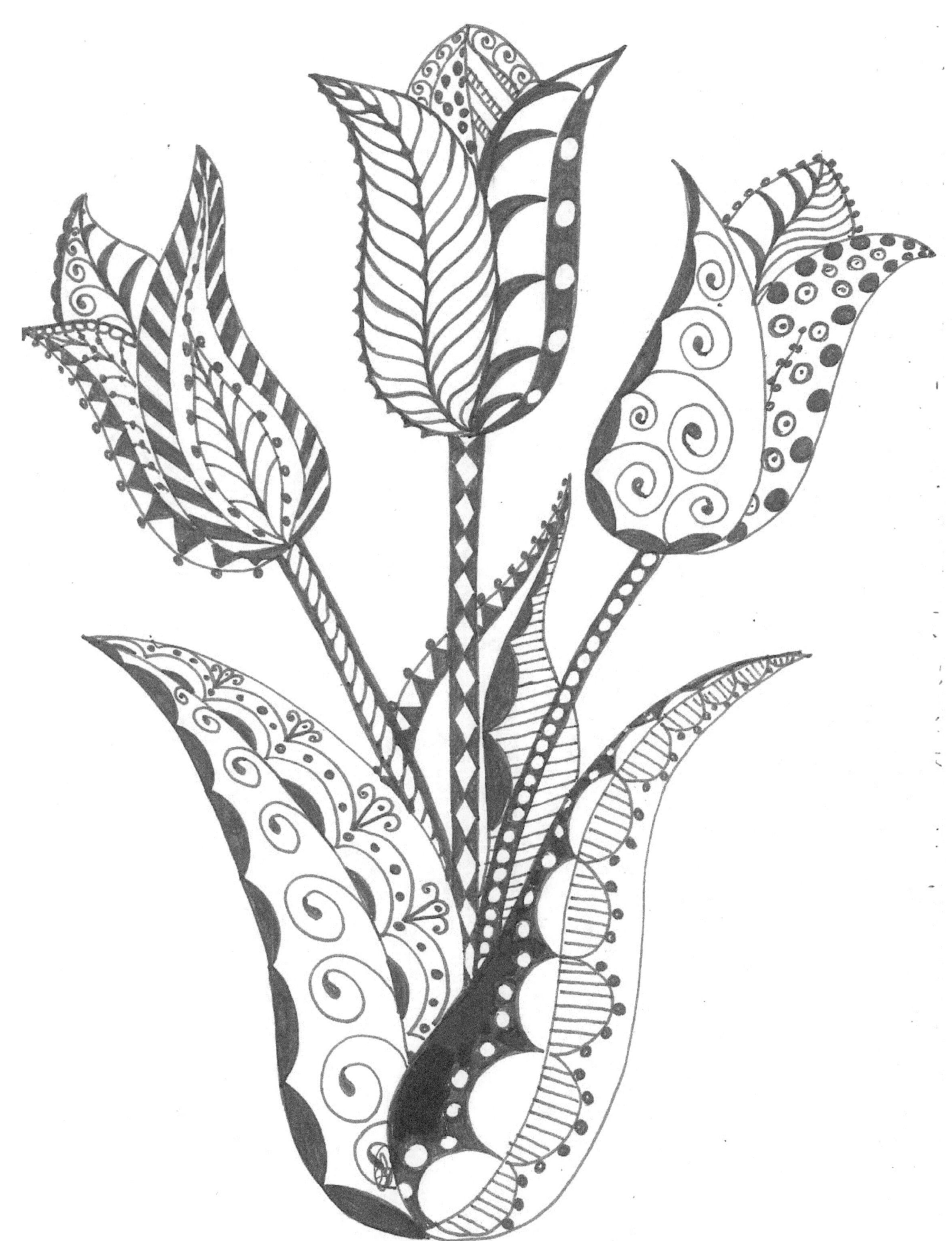

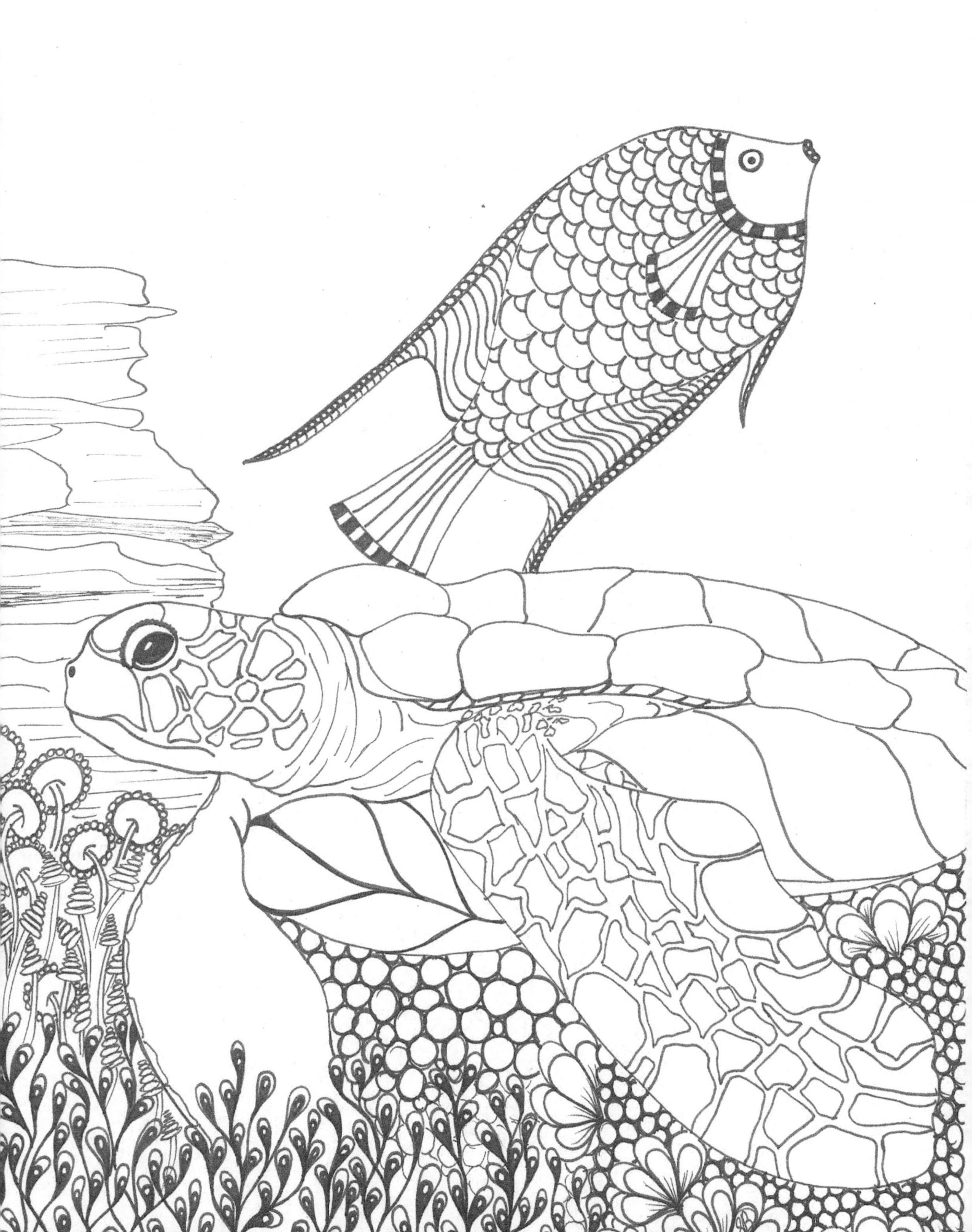

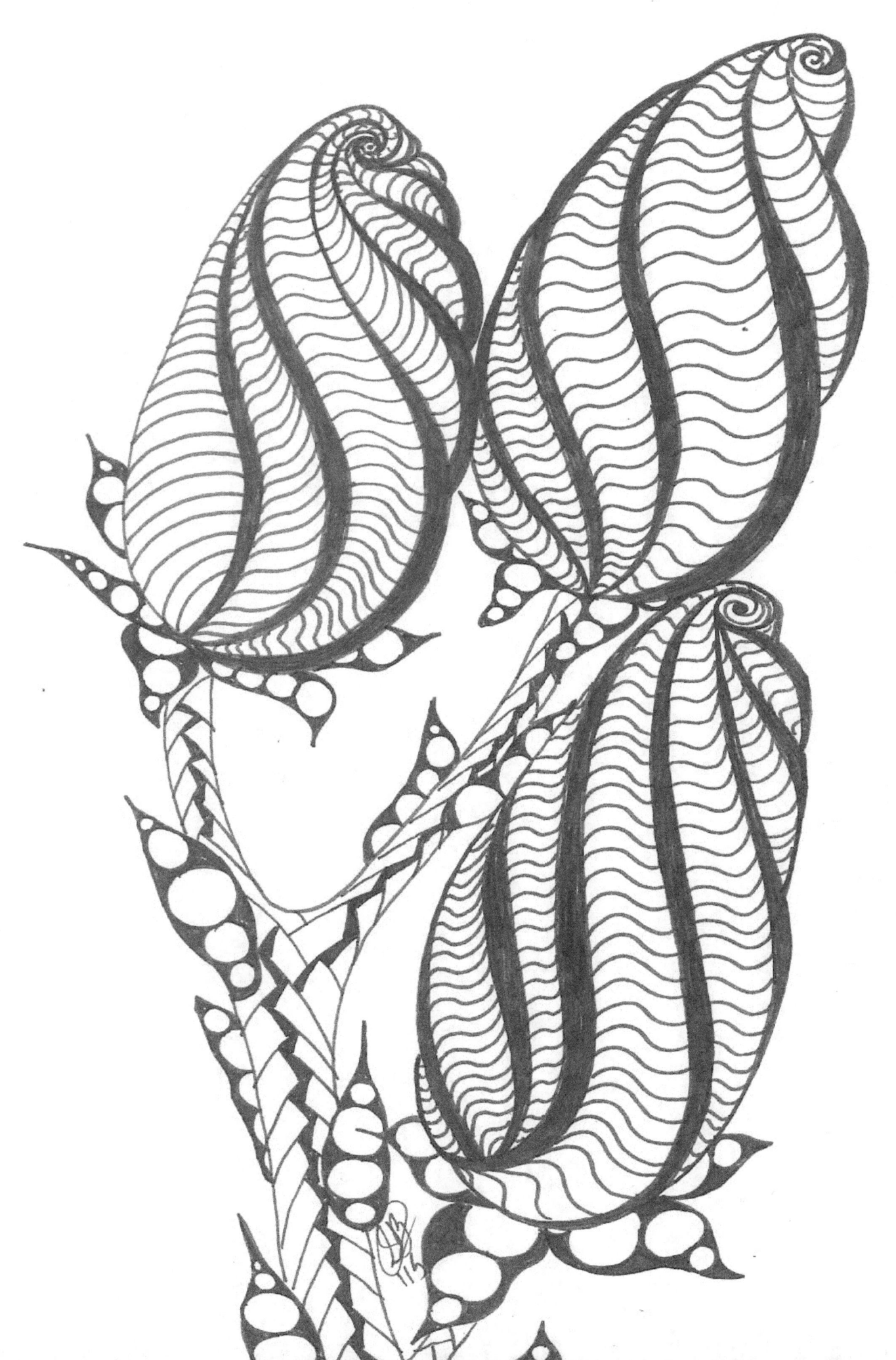

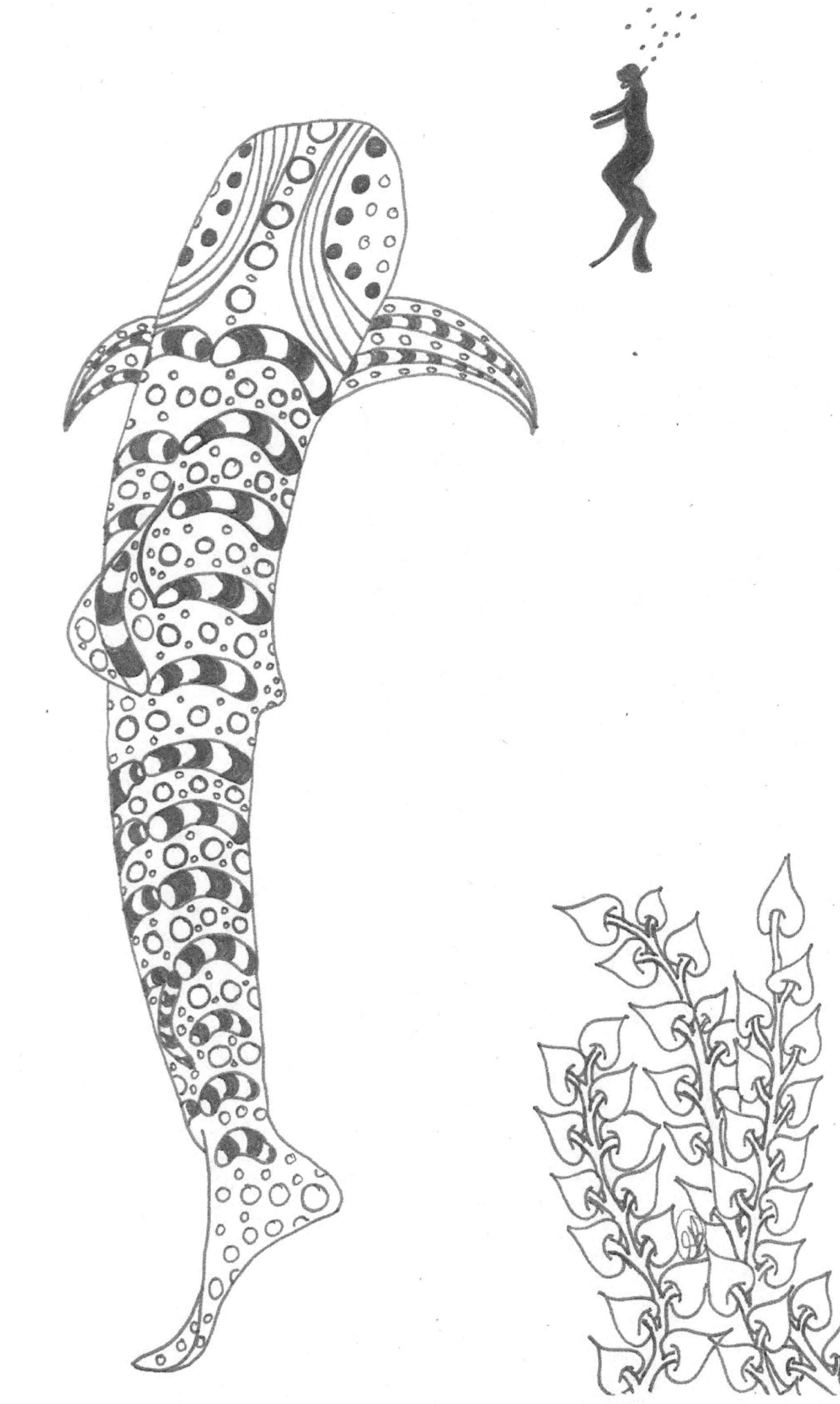

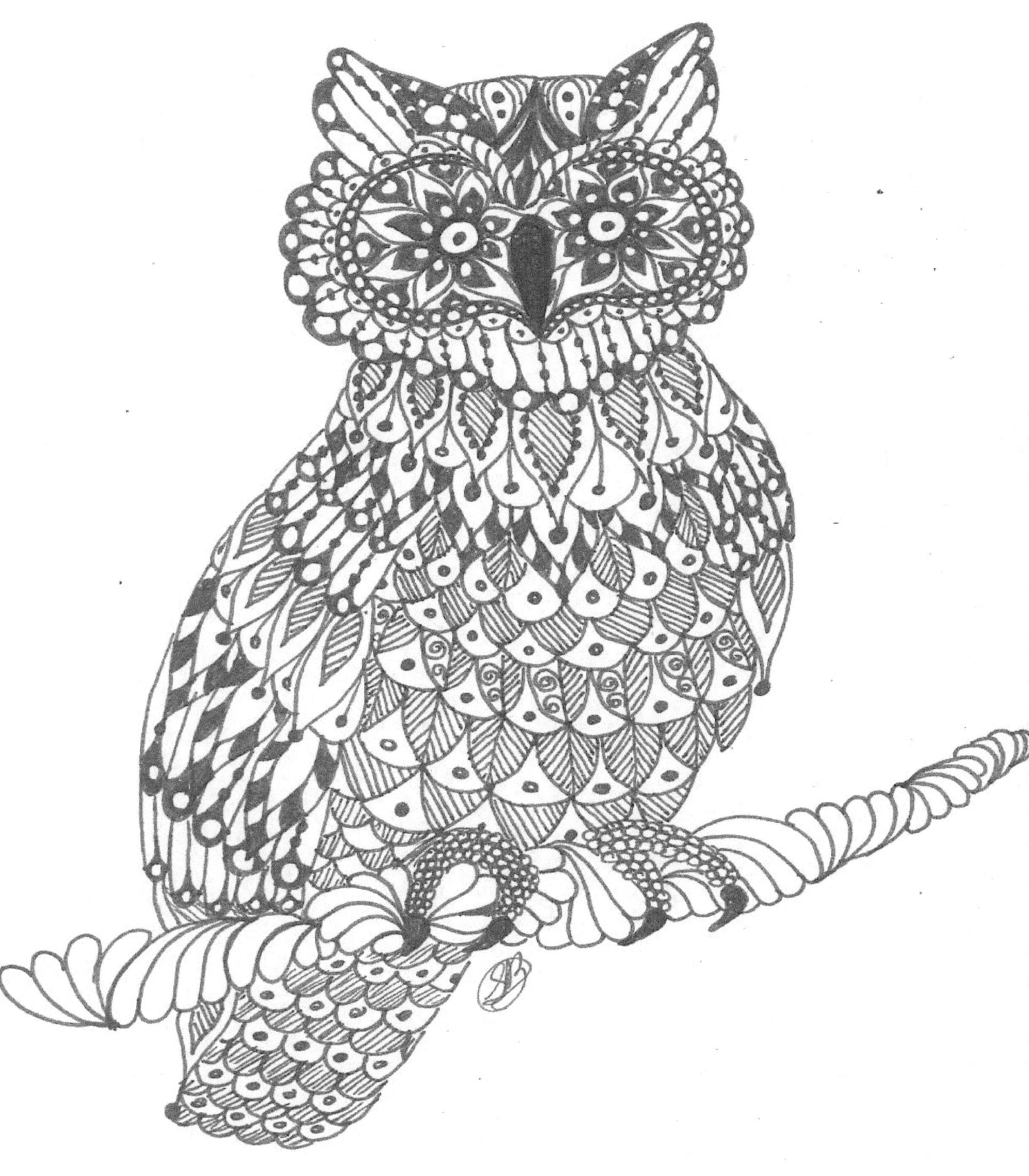

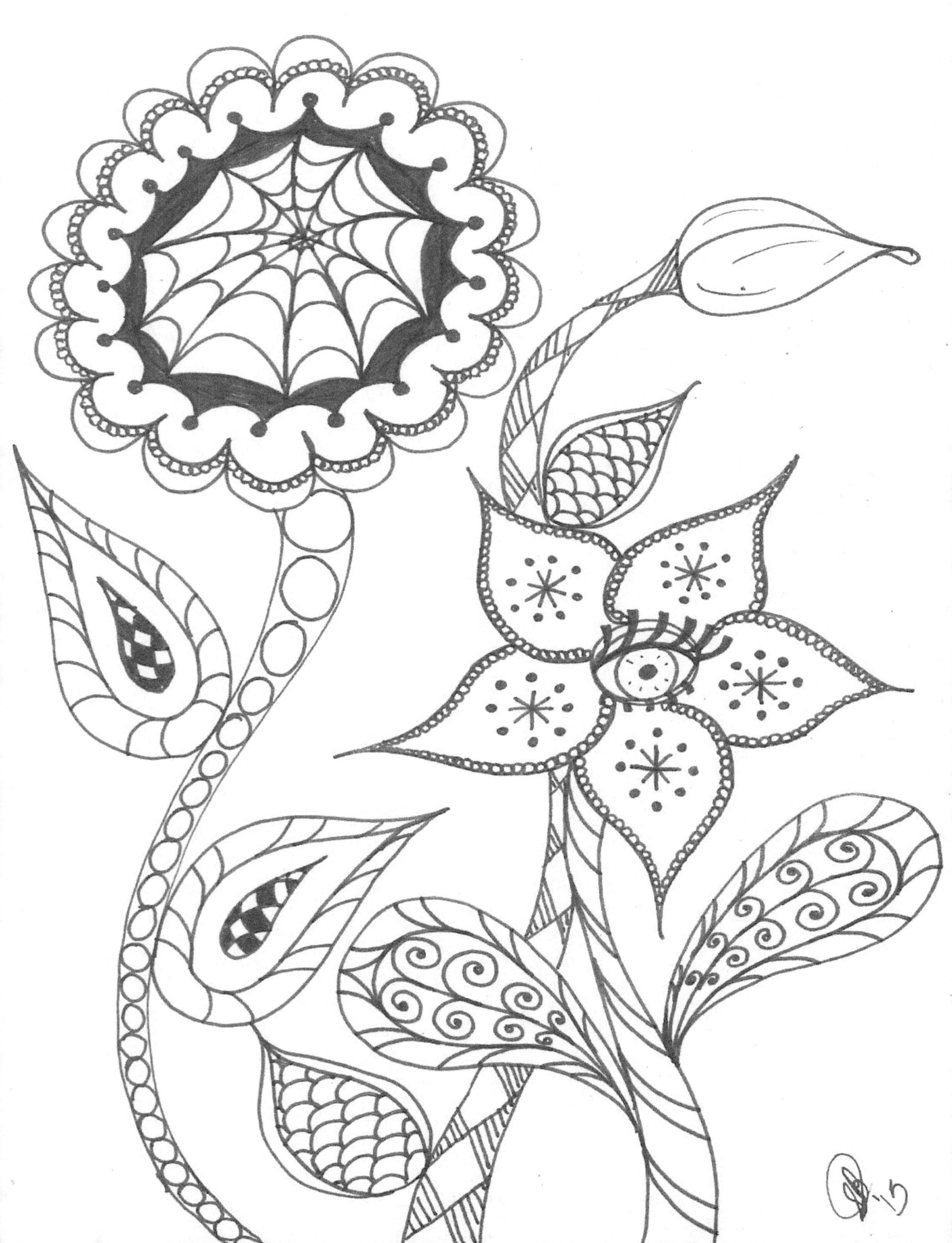

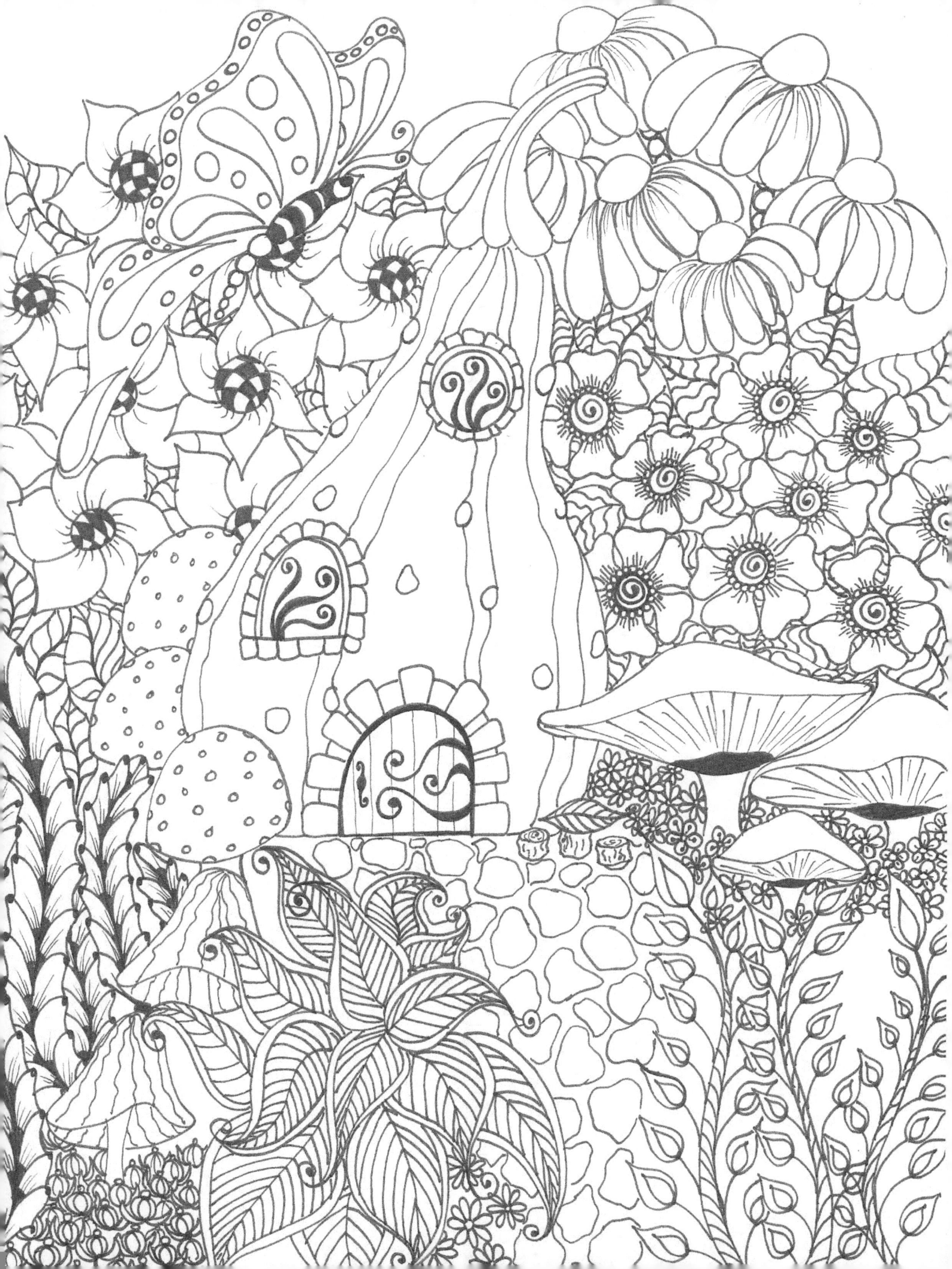

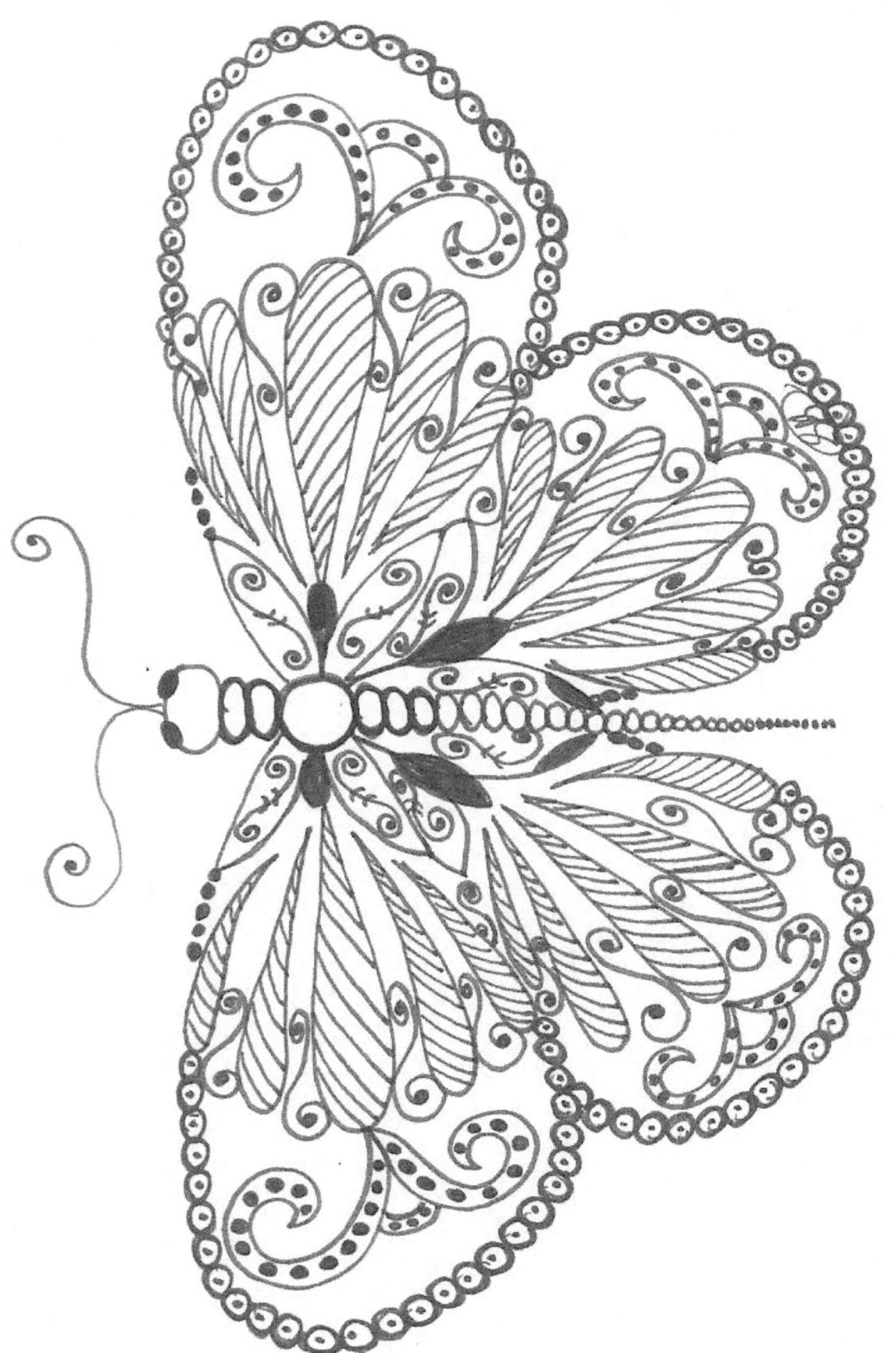

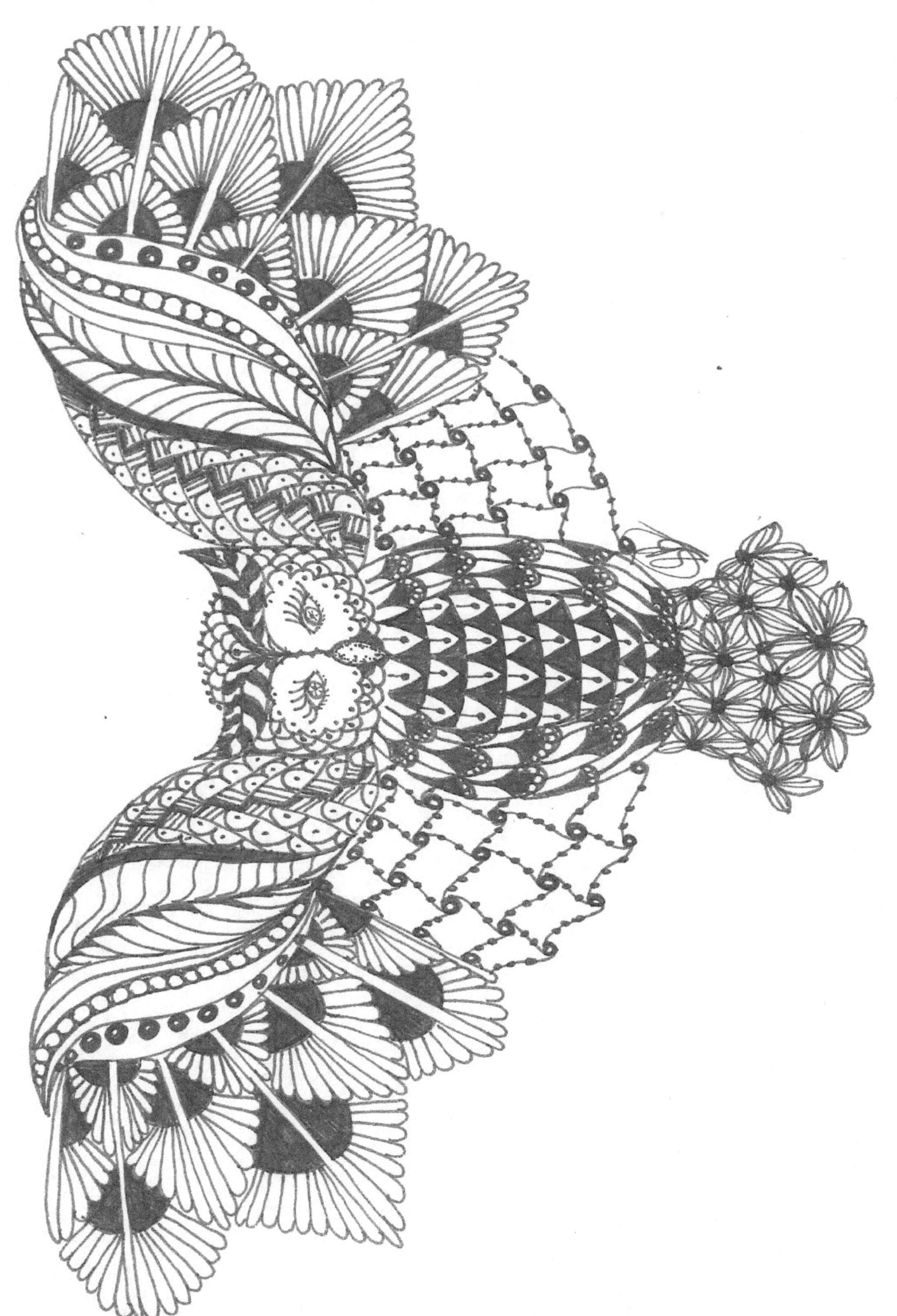

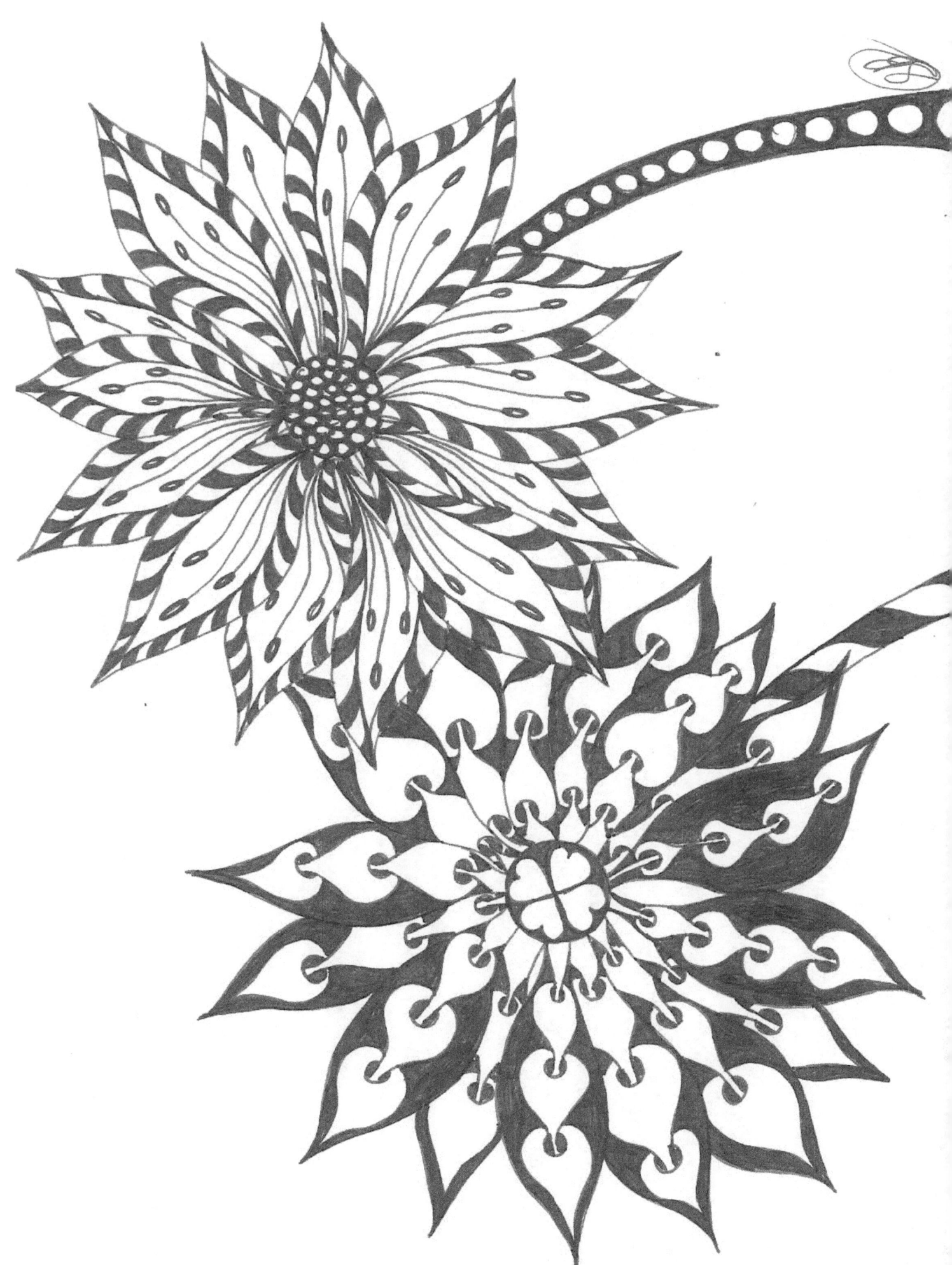

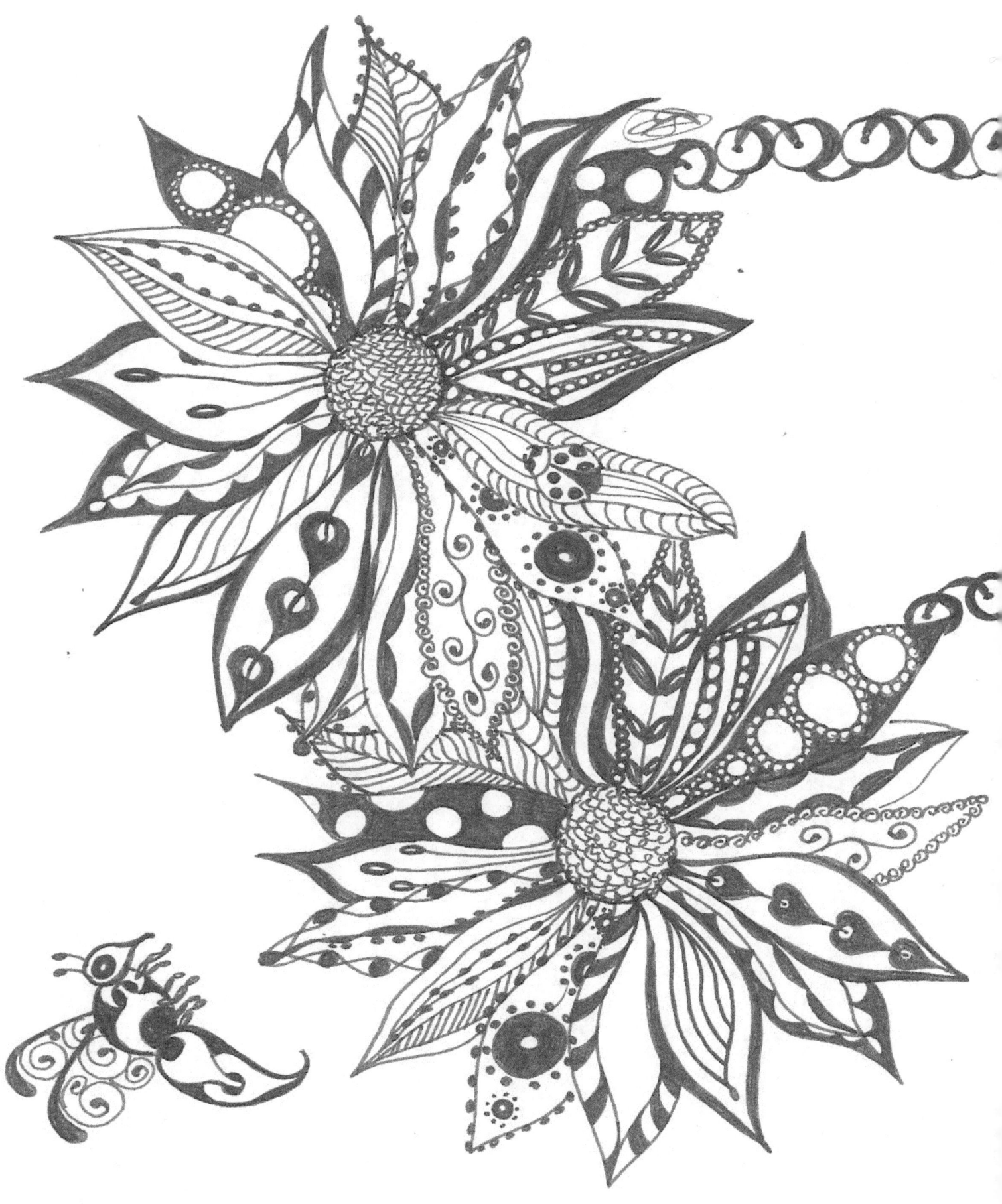

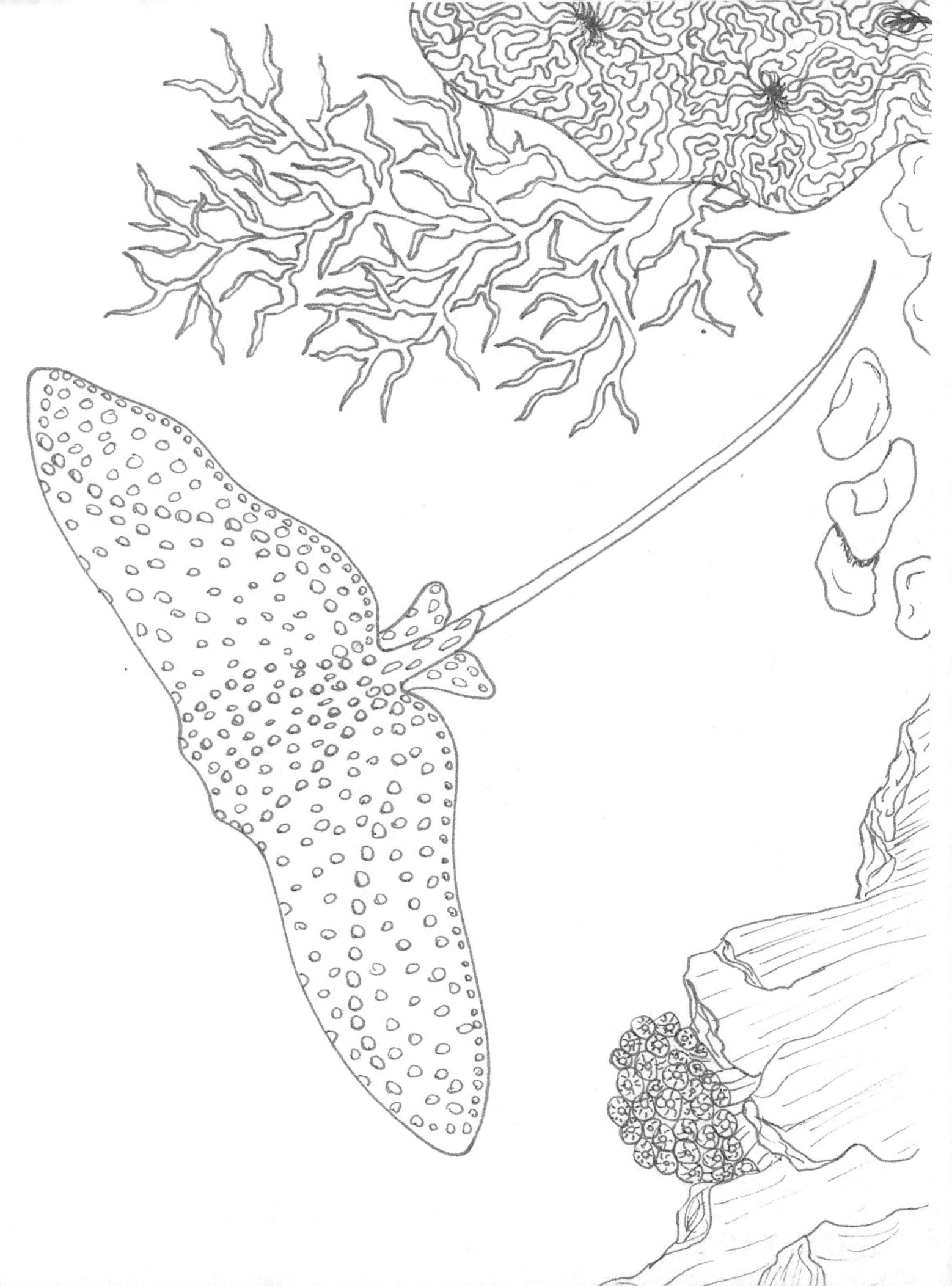

www.ingramcontent.com/pod-product-compliance
Lightning Source LLC
Chambersburg PA
CBHW080607180526
45168CB00007B/2812